Introduction

In Europe, battles of the first World War are ㄱㄷ ㄲㅆㄴㅆㄱㅆ ㅆ ㅕㄷ... trees in ancient forests. But Australia's European settlement is recent, its history almost as barren as its vast interior, so the same events loom much larger. Every year the bravery and sacrifice of the ANZAC troops and those that followed them is celebrated with a national holiday. My first appearance in print was in the 'Brunswick Sentinel', which showed me with 2 other pupils laying wreaths at our school flagpole. Our family told tales of grandfather whose missing toes made him a reject for the Australian army so he stowed away to find his way to the battlefields of France. Eric Bogle's 'The Band Played Waltzing Matilda' told how the war ruined an entire generation, and it became an anthem for our anti-Vietnam War protests.

But until a friend in Bristol, England gave me his grandfather's diary of his time on board HMAS Sydney I, I had never given a thought to the navy's role in the war. I was amazed by his account of the Sydney Emden battle, even more so when further reading filled in the gaps of his account. Edward Bunkin's journal

1

is the inspiration for this book and adds some lucid personal detail to what has been published elsewhere.

Bunkin was a shipwright 2nd class. He signed up for a 2nd 10 year term with the Royal Navy, and on 29 June 1913 joined the Sydney for a 3 year secondment to the Australian navy to deliver and sea test their first light cruiser and later flagship and train the Australian crew. But war broke out and the crew were unexpectedly drawn into the carnage. Bunkin was a lay preacher, and his account is vividly written, but is also infuriating in its omission of what he did, especially during the heat of battle when he was probably repairing damage and possibly helping with the injured. He also omitted the fact that the journey to the colonies was made in company of the new flagship, HMAS Australia which was described by Admiral Graf von Spee as "my special apprehension – she alone is superior to my whole squadron". [1]

His diary is shown in italics. Also noted is an account by Thomas Stevenson, [2] a 17 year old signalman from Sydney who had served on the Tingira, as did Henry Wilson, whose grandson has supplied further information. Sources also include an unnamed officer of the Sydney reported in the London Times, the Captain of the Emden Von Mueller, and the bombastic and romanticised account of Helmuth von Muecke, the Emden's first officer, as well as other sources for clarity.

The extraordinary Sydney-Emden battle proved the proficiency and bravery of Britain's 1st colonial navy, so served as an important morale booster at the start of hostilities, and the bravery of the German crew was acclaimed by both sides. It also signalled the end of the German colonies in Asia, and the career of a raider that had paralysed maritime shipping in the Pacific. Some of the HIGMS Emden's crew were left behind so embarked on an incredible adventure to return to Germany 6 months later. Mexican silver dollars retrieved from the Emden were converted to medals for the Australian crew and to raise funds for the navy; German survivors were permitted to add 'Emden' to their surnames, and subsequent ships of the name still carry the Iron Cross. The battle also harks back to a very different age, when combatants treated each other with great respect, and with great honour. But this battle also involved three groups of men, largely made up of exiles – the Sydney with its colonial melting pot of a crew, the exiles on the Cocos Islands, and the crew of the Emden who were living on borrowed time, with no safe port for respite from their raiding.

Australia became a federal state in 1901 and The Royal Australian Navy was founded in 1909. At the outbreak of war, the RAN was made up of 3,800 , ¼ of whom were on loan from the Royal Navy. This was soon supplemented by a reserve of 493 adults, and 1153 adults and 3093 cadets in training. [3] HMAS Sydney was built at Scotland's Govan shipyards and commissioned at Portsmouth on 29 June 1913. Rear Admiral Stoddard later commented "The Sydney's an ideal ship, the ship I would like to stay in."

Though part of the Australian Navy, the officers remained in the British lists, though the two medical officers were from the RAN. There are some variations in spellings which adds to the confusion as to who was on board at any time. The official crew list is incomplete, giving the names only of British officers and the Australian crew, making a total of 450. Bunkin's name does not appear . Many of the Australians were either young hands or in training. About 60, of which half were boys, were from the Tingira, one of the Australian Navy's first two (sailing) ships. [4] These boys had to be "of very good character and physique" between the ages of 14 and 16. They had been trained on how to work a sailing ship, as well as long route marches with field guns. Its motto was the brutally honest 'learn or leave'.

Australia's population was still largely of British birth or extraction, so lines of nationality were still vague and most still saw Britain as the motherland. This fast new ship, named after the country's first settlement was an important symbol that the offspring was starting to make her way in the world, and served as a model for other British dominions. One account noted after the battle: "the pups have become bulldogs."

The delivery of the two fine ships with their top class crews was very much a promotional and bonding exercise for the empire. This is shown by Bunkin's accounts of the extraordinary welcome she was given in the many ports she visited before the war. She was often open to the public, with up to 2,000 visitors per day, illuminated at night with searchlight displays. Locals held parades, sports days, and regattas in their honour. In Cape Town the crew were showered with wattle, the first they had seen. The Sydney's crew showed they were the equal of the ship, taking more than their share of prizes in swimming, boating and gunnery competitions. When she reached her namesake on 4 October 1913, the event was celebrated with a week's holiday and crowds treated to a parachute display.

She continued her sea trials but on 31 July 1914 the ship arrived in Townsville and heard rumours of war. Four days later England declared war on Germany, and night defences began; the ship's rigging was strengthened and padding put around the bridge and control stations in case of bursting shells

On August 3rd the Federal government offered Britain 20,000 men to serve abroad, and this was immediately organised. [5] With the New Zealanders, his was the first of the AN-ZAC contingents. But the presence of the German warships Emden and Konigsberg in the area and problems in obtaining an escort for them and the New Zealand ships caused repeated delays over the ensuing months. The Prime Minister of Australia, Andrew Fisher "Was a man of extreme caution, and he was intensely anxious not only to give the Empire all possible help, but to prevent any occurrence that might harmfully affect the nerves or zeal of Australians. He had conjured up a picture of 30,000 young untried men afloat, of enemy cruisers dashing in to sink them, of Australia, unused to war, shocked and angered. At so early a stage he felt, the sinking of a transport from preventable causes might push Australia practically out of the war for many months" [6] The Governor General "saw that the Governments of the two Dominions might be constrained by their loyalty to acquiesce n a course which they, and he, believed to be fraught with disastrous possibilities – and all for a strategical (sic) object which seemed to him insignificant as compared with the preservation of the Empire's whole-hearted unity." [7]

On 7 August the Australians were asked by the British to seize the German colonies of Nauru, Caroline Islands and New Guinea to prevent them transmitting information to Admiral Graf von Spee's naval squadron. On 11 August the Sydney joined the destroyers, HMAS Paramatta, Yarra, and Warego to attack New Britain but the German squadron had already left. On 29 August, the Australians, New Zealanders, British and French took Western Samoa in the first coalition action. On 7 September The Sydney became part of the Australian Naval and Military Expeditionary Force which included 1,000 infantry and 2 submarines who destroyed the inland radio station at Rabaul. Crewmembers from the Sydney were involved in fighting locals who stayed loyal to the Germans.

An attack on the wireless station at Bitpaka produced the first Australian casualties of the war. On 14 September The Encounter was the first RAN vessel to fire at an enemy, and conducted the first shore bombardment. Subsequent actions earned the first bravery award and the loss of one of their two submarines with 35 crew. On 26 September the Sydney concluded operations by destroying the wireless station at Anguar in the Palau Islands and checked several islands including Fiji for enemy ships. Meanwhile, other RAN vessels were capturing German merchant shipping.

The destruction of enemy communications was made more urgent by the irresponsible behaviour of Australian newspapers. "Until a severe prohibition was laid upon them, some of the metropolitan papers tried to publish all details of the convoy, its constituent vessels and sailing dates; and at one moment it became necessary to hold up for more than a fortnight all newspapers posted to addresses outside the Commonwealth, lest dangerous disclosures should reach the Dutch Indies and be thence transmitted to the Emden or to other enemy ships." [8]

When preparing for the attack on Rabaul, Sydney's Captain Glossop, aware of his largely young and inexperienced crew, had told them: "*A night attack of this kind requires great nerve on the part of the younger hands and the holding of fire being just as important as the firing. ... No panic must take place and I look to every hand to support each other quickly and quietly, above all no noise. It is of the utmost importance to get back as undamaged as possible as more important work awaits us.*"

ANZAC Escort

This 'more important work' was to escort the first convoy of ANZACs to the Middle East, to fight the Turks for control of the Dardanelles. After months of delays the heavily laden vessels, ranging in speed from 15 to barely 10 knots departed from Albany, Western Australia on November 1.

It was a *magnificent sight, 38 transports with men, horses, food, ammunition and everything they require as a fighting force. Twelve ships from New Zealand and 26 ships from Australia of the largest and fastest boats we have and to escort them is HMS Minotaur (Flagship China Station) HMAS Melbourne and HMAS Sydney.* On board the HMAT Afric was 2nd lieutenant Alfred Shout, whose bravery was later recognised by being posthumously awarded the Victoria Cross, making him the most decorated soldier at Gallipoli. [9]

6

Ibuki, the Japanese battleship joined them later, escorting two more transports from Fremantle. The Japanese had been important as allies in helping to clear the Germans from the islands and had taken possession of their colonies north of the Equator whilst the British claimed those to the south. This also deprived the German navy of their safe ports, forcing Von Spee's squadron to withdraw from the area. Only the SMS Emden remained, without radar she was untraceable so the region was on full alert. "So the great fleet, comprising 4 warships with 38 transports in charge, voyaged towards its tiny enemy like an elephant timidly approaching the dreaded mouse. No more conspicuous example could be given or imagined of naval power and its limitations, of the overwhelming need of warships to the Empire, and its defencelessness without their dominance throughout the oceans. One enemy cruiser, smaller and weaker than any of the four in the convoy's escort, could force not only the use of all the 4, but the spreading over the Indian Ocean of 9 more: for at this moment the Japanese 'Yagagi' and 'Chikuma', the Russian 'Askold', and the British 'Hampshire', 'Yarmouth', 'Weymouth', 'Gloucester', 'Empress of Russia', and 'Empress of Asia' were all being directed on 'The Emden', while other Japanese warships were drawing down towards the southern and western sea-passages of the Malay Archipelago." [10]

Four days later the convoy was overtaken by the mail steamer SS Osterly with £2,000,000 bullion on board. On November 8, following the disastrous Battle of Coronel off South Africa when Von Spee's squadron sank the HMS Monmouth and HMS Good Hope, all efforts were put into hunting down the German squadron. The Minotaur was called away to help with the South African Rebellion and Melbourne took command at the head of the convoy, leaving no guard on the rear.

Early on 9 November as the convoy steamed to the south west of Java en route to Colombo, the quiet day was disturbed by a wireless message from Cocos (Keeling) Islands warning of the approach of a strange warship, with a fake funnel which was soon confirmed as the SMS Emden. The Germans had destroyed all other communication links with Australia, leaving their Direction Island with the only intact undersea cable to South Africa and Singapore.

The Minotaur turned back, but was too far away to help. Melbourne increased her speed and prepared to investigate, but realizing his responsibilities at the head of the convoy, her captain returned to his position and signalled Sydney, the closest to the Cocos, to investigate. [11] When the Sydney reported sighting an enemy cruiser, The Melbourne moved from her position at the head of the convoy to the south west, nearest to the danger and "..called the *Ibuki* to join her. The *Ibuki* was by no means willing to do this; she too had received the *Sydney's* message and at once hoisted all her battle-flags, cleared for action, and started at full speed to follow the *Sydney* but the safety of the convoy was the primary consideration." [12]

The Germans had, quite reasonably, expected the wireless station to be heavily defended. One author claimed "Under the direction of the British Admiralty, a network of French, Russian, Japanese and British warships had been spread over a vast area, portion of the cordon consisting of the commonwealth cruisers Sydney and Melbourne. ....it becomes necessary to set a trap which will tempt the pirate-vessel into striking distance. The Admiralty decides to offer a rich bait, the Cocos Island cable station." [13] The trap was so cunning that nobody on either side knew of it. Either lack of manpower or simply confusion of the early months of the war left the Island defenceless. The large and vulnerable ANZAC squadron was poorly defended; when the Sydney left they were even more at risk. Had the Emden or any other enemy ship found the troop convoy and got in amongst them, they could have caused the most horrendous carnage in the crowded troop carriers, and the defending ships would have been helpless to retaliate for fear of harming their own.

8

One of the Emden's officers later claimed "We should have got in among the transports from astern, and slipped into the first division astern of the 3rd and 4th ship; then we should have done all possible damage with our guns and torpedoes, and we should certainly have sunk half a dozen ships – probably 12 – before your escort could have come up and stopped us." [14] But this was clearly written after the event, as "We now know that a raid into Australian waters was only one of the less important of the possible tasks laid down for the German squadron, and that it had been discarded by Von Spee, who – it is practically certain – was unaware of the existence of the contingents. But, had he heard even as much as subsequently did the *Emden,* his decision might have been different." [15] The Germans had mocked the military capacity of the British colonies, so they may well have underestimated their importance. In view of the following events, there must have been a certain poetic justice felt by the victors.

The Emden

The SMS Emden was a light cruiser commissioned for the Imperial German Navy in 1910, and started with a crew of 361. The captain was anglophile Captain Karl Friederich Max Von Mueller. Her first officer Helmuth von Muecke later published bombastic and highly romaticised accounts both of the Emden and of his adventure packed journey back to Germany. Their second torpedo officer was Prince Hohenzollern, nephew of the Kaiser. Their second officer Witthoefft became Captain of the 2nd Emden, One survivor claimed "The old Emden was manned by Germany's choicest men. Physical sturdiness, an unblemished reputation, and a high efficiency rating were the requirements the men met." [16]

At the outbreak of war, von Spee's squadron decided to head for the South Atlantic, but von Mueller was given permission to became a lone raider, intent on inflicting as much damage as possible on British shipping. Her career began on September 10th when she began hunting on some of the world's busiest and most important trade routes.

In the absence of modern technology, it was impossible to predict her movements, but this worked both ways, as von Muecke wrote: "We knew quite well that 16 hostile ships were in pursuit of us – British, French and Japanese. We never had any information with regard to the position of these ships, nor of their character, which, after all, could matter very little to us, since the Emden was the smallest and least formidable of all the war ships in the Indian Ocean. There was not a hostile cruiser, that she was likely to meet, that was not her superior in strength. That the Emden's career must soon be cut short was therefore a prospect of which everyone aboard her felt certain. Many hounds are certain death to the hare....There was not a port where we could put in to make repairs, and vacancies that might occur in the personnel could not be filled in any case. Our commander had set this aspect of affairs before us, sharply and clearly, at the very outset of the Emden's career, pointing out that the only future ahead of the Emden was to inflict as much damage as possible upon the enemy before she herself should be destroyed, which, in any event, could be but a question of time." [17]

Von Muecke suggests the career was both planned and accepted by the crew, but when they were told of Japan's entry to the war on the 26th of August, there seems to have been less clarity, as a crew member recalled:. ".. we all thought it was now quite impossible for Germany to win with three Great Powers attacking us. When the news had been announced, a voice from the back said, "Where are we and the *Emden* going?" "I don't know myself; but first we'll get some provisions out of the English." [18]

At this time, the Indian Ocean carried so much British Empire shipping it was sometimes called an English Lake. Ships were dependent on bulky coal for fuel, the best of which came from South Wales. Having an enemy raider on the loose was a terrifying prospect, threatening to bring the Empire to a standstill, forcing up insurance premiums with ships afraid to take to sea, and putting ports at risk. This is why the colonial navies had gone to such efforts to hunt down and purge the Germans from the islands of South East Asia, causing von Spee's flight.

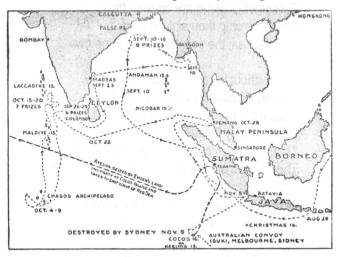

When The Emden left the main squadron, she embarked on an extraordinarily destructive, but short career. Repeatedly crossing some of the most frequented shipping lanes in the world,

11

she attacked merchant shipping, sinking those of the enemy and using captured neutral ships to convey victims to safety, whilst keeping herself unhurt and undiscovered. In a mere 6 weeks she had captured or sunk 21 vessels, of about 100,000 tons, bombarded the oil depot at Madras and attacked warships in Penang Harbour. Both sites were undefended and the Russian light cruiser Zemchung's captain was later court martialled and imprisoned for 3 ½ years for gross negligence.[19]. Emden was so active and pervasive she gained the nickname of 'The Flying Dutchman' and inspired an impressive piece of poetry, written by one of her reservist officers, whilst in a Singapore gaol. [20] or by Maria Weinand [21]

Ship without harbour, knowing no ease,
Emden flying over the seas –
German laurel is wound round thy mast,
Curses of England are chasing thee fast;
Ship after ship thou sinkest alone,
And the sea, the sea, the sea is thine own.

Ship without harbour, knowing no ease,
Glorious Emden, pride of the seas –
Thou has succumbed to an enemy's blow?
Destroyed by flames – the work of the foe?
Thou has been sunk in the depth of the sea?
Thou – thou art dead? Nay, that can never be!

Ship without harbour, knowing no ease
Unforgettable queen of he seas!
Emden, thou never, never canst die:
Over the seas thy shadow will fly,
Ever to make the enemy quail,
Ever in German hearts to sail!

Whoever wrote it, this piece of bloated Romanticism still stands up better than the Admiralty Laureate, Sir Henry Newbolt shows as little understanding of the battle as he did of natural history when describing the crew of the Sydney:

"their hearts were hot, and as they shot,
they sang like kangaroos!" [22].

But the usually boastful von Muecke is dismissive of the reputation they acquired: "It has been frequently said by the English that it was wholly due to her great speed that the Emden remained afloat as long as she did. This is not the case. Aside from the fact that the ship's bottom was so heavy with barnacles etc. that the Emden could not run at her highest speed, she could at no time make more than 11 nautical miles on an average, for the very good reason that the coal tenders, on which she was dependent for fuel, could travel no faster. Moreover, a greater speed would have profited us little. Whereas, at a speed of eleven miles, we found it possible to avoid a hostile encounter, we might, by the greater rate of twenty miles an hour, have rushed straight upon the enemy." [23]

He also delighted in listing the prizes they took, including live animals and many luxury items, though their definition of necessities included soda water. They also obtained fire bricks for their chief engineer, to protect the mostly wooden ship from their furnaces. [24] Their men were probably the best fed mariners that had ever existed. They were also perhaps the cleanest and best entertained."...a large number of shower baths, made out of old pipes, had been arranged up on deck. The entire crew had a shower bath 3 times a day, each man being allowed to enjoy it as long as he liked.

The state of health upon the Emden was excellent. From the time we left Tsingtao until the day of our encounter with the Sidney (sic), there was not a case of sickness on board.

Every afternoon the ship's band gave us quite a long concert. At such times, the men all sat cosily about on the forecastle, listening to the music, some joining in with their voices, while others smoked or danced. In the evening after darkness had set in, the singers aboard usually got together, and then every possible and impossible song was sung by a chorus that was excellent both in volume and quality."[25]

But von Muecke had previously described a totally different, far more exhausting, stressful and ultimately more realistic life. He writes of the constant stream of ships to be captured, unloaded, people sent to safe ports in neutral ships whilst the enemy shipping was sunk. "These days were strenuous ones for our men, as the war watch was continued without intermission, in order that the ship might be ready at a moment's notice for any emergency. There was no opportunity to give the crew even a short season of rest. For us, there was not one harbour of refuge where we might lie free from danger." [26]

Bunkin's diary goes into great detail about the time taken for loading coal, and of the clean up afterwards, which was hard enough in a safe port, but at sea was much more difficult and dangerous. Von Muecke writes of how the endless coaling damaged the ship "Ere long there was not an undamaged railing post on the entire starboard side. The linoleum deck also suffered greatly. Soon it was worn through. There were large holes in it, which laid bare the polished steel deck beneath. This, in itself, was of little consequence, but the places where the steel was exposed were so smooth that, especially at night, and when the ship rolled badly, the men often slipped on it and fell. For this reason, as soon as we had finished coaling, men were set to work at roughening the steel surface wherever it was exposed. To this end we used chisels, with which we cut narrow grooves into the steel, thereby giving the men a firmer hold for their feet. Somewhat later, after one of the English steamers had provided us with a large quantity of tar and some very strong sail-cloth, we covered the deck with this." [27]

Captain von Mueller claimed his goal in attacking the Cocos Islands was, "Apart from the material damage the enemy would have suffered by the destruction of the cable and wireless stations and the temporary interruption of telegraphic communications between Australia on the one hand and England and other countries on the other, I hoped also to effect (1) a general unrest among shipping to and from Australia by creating the impression that The *Emden* would proceed to harry the steamer traffic south and west of Australia, and (2) a withdrawal from the Indian Ocean of at least some of the English cruisers which were taking part in the hunting down of the *Emden*. My intention was, after carrying out the raid on the Cocos group, to make for Socotra and cruise in the gulf of Aden, and then on the steamer-route between Aden and Bombay." [28] Which is interesting as he made no mention of the ANZAC convoy, but was solely interested in merchant shipping. Though he had heard of its existence by this time, Von Mueller assumed it would head straight across the Indian Ocean, further south, if it dared to sail at all. The convoy chose to avoid the mail steamer route, and was due to pass Cocos near dawn on November 9th, about 50 miles to the east. [29]

Unfortunately for Von Mueller, his understanding of his opponents was massively flawed: no nation would abandon essential shipping when the enemy was harassing it; a more likely response was to increase efforts to hunt down the raider. The more active the Emden became, the more likely she was to be caught.

The Emden arrived on the evening of 7 November about 30 miles north of North Keeling Island and the following morning loaded up with coal from commandeered collier with German crew, the Exford who then vanishes from this story. Their other collier The Bueresk was at the Cocos Islands with orders to be abandoned if a hostile ship was sighted. [30] The crew of the Emden was thus depleted before the battle began.

Von Mueller recorded that the Cocos Islands began sending out an hourly message; by dawn on the 8th a British warship replied, but her signal strength decreased, as her distance increased. The code for the ship was NC so she assumed her to be the Newcastle, (it was The Minotaur) and he assumed it was en route to the Cape Colony rebellion. Running low on coal, he considered a further delay, but when the messages died out he assumed the area was clear of the enemy so decided to risk an attack on Cocos. [31] This delay ensured she was still there when the Sydney arrived.

The Battle

When most of us think of sea battles, we usually imagine old paintings of sailing ships lined up blasting each other to pieces. This battle was of an entirely different nature "...even the modern battle between fleets, in which there is comparatively small scope for manoeuvre, differed almost *in toto* from the single-ship action between fast cruisers, in which each has the utmost freedom of manoeuvre and the movements of each are frequently obscured from the other by drifting smoke. It must also be clearly and persistently remembered that the fight now described began while the combatants were nearly 6 miles apart; that during the actual fight

16

they were never closer than 3 miles; and that even at the last, when the *Emden* was ashore and the *Sydney* stood in to compel her to lower her flag, they were separated by a good deal more than 2 miles." [32]

From the outset, mistakes were made as to the identities of the various ships. When the Emden was first sighted, the residents of Direction Island in the Cocos group thought she had 4 funnels so assumed she was British, probably the Minotaur who they knew to be in the region.

The Sydney could not at first tell whether the ship they sighted was the Emden or the Koenigsburg, both of which were thought to be in the region, but knew she was faster than both, so slowed her approach to prepare for battle.

Apparently when von Mueller first sighted the smoke of Sydney's funnel approaching, he assumed it was the Bueresk, but "soon began to doubt.. as she was usually almost smokeless; but it was considered that the unusually dense smoke-cloud might be attributed to her having had a fire in her bunkers the day before, which was probably causing her to use the partly burnt coal; moreover she would certainly be running at top speed." [33]

"When, however, the signaller reported a four-funnelled ship, he knew her to be a British cruiser – but, believing the Australians ships to be many miles off to the south-west, took her for the Newcastle or a sister-ship, nearer his own size and age. Consequently he determined to fight her. [34] This contradicts von Mueller's earlier claim that the Emden was the smallest ship in the war,

As the Sydney rushed into battle, exceeding her estimated top speed of 25 knots, "Captain Glossop at the compass on the fore-bridge, his navigating lieutenant (Lieutenant Rahilly who was in control of the guns throughout the action) close by, ready to "spot" with his binoculars the fall of shot: the paymaster on deck, sitting on the ship's box of confidential papers and ready to throw them overboard if anything went wrong with the *Sydney*;

every other officer and man at his fighting station." [35]

An officer on the Sydney writing for The Times of London was in the bath when notified of the enemy and thought it was a joke. Once he realised the ship was gaining speed, he called for the barber to cut his hair, amidst much bandinage from his mates. Bunkin, like many of the crew, had never seen action, and his journal captures the excitement:

It is easy to know we are increasing speed as the ship almost seems to be like a dog at a lease (sic) and trying to get away. First a slight heave and then settle down and up again and the white foam is shot up on both sides of us and our wake is simply one mass of boiling foam.

'Cooks' is sounded off and we all go to breakfast. Immediately after breakfast is cleared away everyone is wondering what the next few hours will bring forth, the look out in the Crow's Nest (a barren spot nearly at the top of the mast) reports smoke ahead and almost immediately the bell is told (sic) for church and everyone goes aft. As soon as church is over 'Action' is sounded off.

During this time we have been closing on the object and it is seen a ship is trying to escape but before 'Clear for Action' is completed it is seen the ship has turned round and making for us and just as everyone had got to his allotted station for General Quarters (that is closed up around the guns and torpedo tubes etc) the ship opened fire on us 9.40am.

We immediately replied but it must be acknowledged the enemy's first shots were very accurate. The first shots (salvo) carrying away our Foremast Rangefinder and killing the operator, this putting the gunlayers off their aim for a few moments but they soon picked up the enemy's ship individually and was not long before we could see our shots were getting home and telling on the enemy, their firing became more erratic.

This early success for the Emden was partly due to an element of surprise in being able to fire at an elevation of 30 degrees whereas the British guns could only rise to 18. This difference was unknown to Captain Glossop, [36] but it is to his credit

18

how quickly he and his crew responded to the damage and were soon in charge of the action.

The Times' officer noted "The hottest part of the action for us was the first half hour....The men are splendid at loading drill, but to practise supply of ammunition is almost impossible in peace time. To have a big supply stacked on the upper deck is far too dangerous a proceeding in action, and what with getting an even distribution of projection and cartridges between the two guns, getting the safety caps off, with fiddly pins and things to take out, attending to misfires, cheering up the one or two who seemed to be "pulling dry", you can imagine I had little time to be thinking much about the Emden" [37]

He wrote that when the control position was knocked out, all were injured which he considered very lucky. He regretted not having time to get cotton wool, and had become deaf. "Coming aft ... I was met by a lot of men cheering and waving their caps. I said, "What's happened?" "She's gone, Sir, she's gone." I ran to the ship's side, and no sign of a ship could I see. If one could have seen a dark cloud of smoke, it would have been different. But I could see nothing. So I called out, "All hands turn out the life-boats, there will be men in the water." They were just starting to do this when someone called out, "She's still firing, Sir," and every one ran back to the guns. What had happened was a cloud of yellow or very light coloured smoke had obscured her from view... By now her 3 funnels and her foremast had been shot away, and she was on fire aft. We turned again and after giving her a salvo or two with the starboard guns saw her run ashore on north Keeling Island. So at 11.20 am we ceased firing, the action having lasted 1 hour 40 minutes."

Captain von Mueller's report is just as calm as the above, but makes for far more dramatic reading. Within about 15 minutes of the start of the battle, a shell had splintered near the conning tower, injuring the gunnery officer, the torpedo officer who was also acting manoeuvring officer, and the seaman operating the engine room telegraph and ordnance artificer transmitting orders

19

to the guns, the latter 2 having to leave the conning tower. Five minutes later the steering gear had failed and most of that section dead, so crewmen went forward to operate it. But a direct hit on their ammunition had already taken out the gear, starting a fire so these crewmen could not return. Soon after this, several crew were blown overboard by an exploding shell. The ship could only be steered by her screws and their range finders failed. Their firing was dying down due to serious casualties of gunners and loaders, and the torpedo air compressor was out of action. Speaking tubes were badly damaged, so communication was almost impossible – the noise prevented shouting orders. Two funnels were knocked over, and when the third fell overboard it took with it an officer and crewman from the crow's nest.

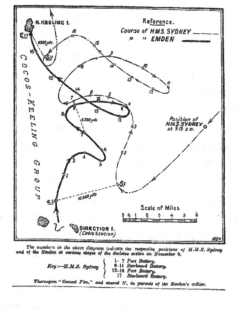

This would have been more than enough to make most people put up the white flag, but von Mueller was determined to fire a torpedo, though was hampered by the lack of speed. Without the funnels, the remaining furnace doors had to be left open to avoid danger from gas and smoke. Soon after, he was informed that an underwater leak had caused the abandonment of the torpedo room, so the Emden could no longer do any harm to their opponent. It was only then that von Mueller decided to wreck his ship on the reef of North Keeling Island to prevent further loss of his crew.

He wrote: "Shortly before grounding, which happened about 11.15 am, I had both engines stopped; immediately after the impact I ordered "Full speed ahead" again so as to jam the ship on the reef as thoroughly as possible. Then I ordered fires to be drawn in all boilers, and all the engine and boiler rooms to be flooded; also, as the *Sydney* at first continued firing, I gave permission to everyone on deck, or who came on deck, to drop overboard and swim to the island....several men had jumped overboard and reached the shore about 100 yards away through the surf. Some it seems were unfortunately drowned in the attempt; others were pulled on board again from the water after the *Sydney* stopped firing. An attempt was then made by paying out a line to establish a hawser communication with the island, in order, by means of a breeches-buoy, to transfer to the shore the personnel still left on board, together with provisions and drinking water. But all attempts to effect this, both on this and the following day, failed because the strong current setting across prevented floats from reaching the shore, while the line usually got hooked behind coral-rocks, and then broke." [38]

From the telegraph station on Direction Island the battle could be watched from the roofs of the huts; locals saw the Sydney disappear in a pall of black smoke when her range finder was hit, and believed her lost until she recommenced firing. They described the Emden, generally the nearer of the two, as "a splendid picture in her light grey paint, standing out smoke free, and clear-cut against the blue background of the ocean: spitting viciously like a wild cat as our shells fell all around her and sent up huge white-crested columns."[39] This also points to another difference between the two ships: the raider was using best quality coal from South Wales, whereas the Sydney was using more smoky and less efficient Australian fuel.

The Times Correspondent claimed the Emden began shooting when the Sydney could just see her funnels, so he estimated to be 12 miles distant. The battle followed a complicated course, as shown on the map, with the Emden repeatedly trying to get under the range of the Sydney's guns .

With the Emden disabled, Bunkin recorded at 11.20 am: *Finding she could do no more damage we then went after the collier that was supplying her with coal and during the action tried to escape. We soon overtook her 12.00 noon and by firing a shot across her bows made her stop. A boarding party was then sent aboard but found the German Officers had put her into a sinking position by damaging the underwater valves beyond repair. We then made all prisoners and transferred them aboard the Sydney – officers 3, German sailors 16, English cooks detained 2, Chinese crew also taken off. Our captain then gave orders to load 1 of the guns (and) fired 4 shots into the collier to help her on her downward journey to Davey Jones locker... the collier before being captured by the Germans was English and left Newcastle for Malay Straits with a cargo of coal and named SS Buresk.*

After we got the prisoners on board and found the collier going down rapidly we then returned to Keeling Island where we found the Emden still flying the "German Ensign" also a distress signal so our Captain made a signal to the Emden and told them to haul down their Ensign which to all appearance was ignored so the Captain sent for one of the German Officers (prisoners from the Buresk) and (he) was brought up under armed guard. He then asked, if he sent them over if their Capt would surrender on condition of taking all on board, but they point blank said he would not surrender at any cost. So our captain said he would have no alternative but to open fire again which he did at 4.25 pm and ceased

4.30 doing further considerable damage and carrying away (as estimated by the prisoners later) between 60 and 70 men. By this time a white Flag was showing and not long after it was seen one of the men was scaling the main rigging and in a very few minutes the German Ensign hauled down.

Captain Glossop's version is that when he returned to the *Emden*, "She still had her colours up at mainmast head. I enquired by signal international code, "Will you surrender?" and received a reply in Morse "What signal?" "No signal books" then made in Morse, "Do you surrender?" and subsequently "Have you received my signal?" to neither of which did I get an answer. The German officers on board gave me to understand that the captain would never surrender, and therefore, though very reluctantly, I again fired at her 4.30 pm, ceasing at 4.35pm as she showed white flags and hauled down her ensign by sending a man aloft." [40]

This final salvo from the Sydney is possibly one of the reasons this incident is less famous than it would otherwise deserve. It seems Capt Glossop opened fire on a defenceless enemy, but he was only following the rules of engagement.

Von Mueller's account tells a slightly different story: "About 4pm the *Sydney* was again sighted to the westward. As she had two boats in tow, we imagined that she intended taking the survivors on board. When a fairly long distance from the *Emden* the boats were cast loose, and the *Sydney* steamed past the *Emden's* stern at a distance of about 4,300 yards. As she had international signals flying I sent a Morse message by flag – "No signal–book aboard", for our signal-book had been burnt. When the *Sydney* had passed our stern and lay aft on our starboard quarter, she opened fire again unexpectedly with several salvoes, by which several of my men were killed or wounded, and fresh fires were started. I again gave the crew leave to abandon ship if they could swim and wanted to, as I did not know how long the *Sydney* would go on firing, and this seemed to be the only possibility of escape. A number of the crew went overboard, some reached the island, some were drowned in the attempt, some were afterwards dragged back on board. As the *Emden* was now incapable of fighting, and lay a helpless wreck on a coral reef, I ordered a white flag to be shown in token that the rest of the crew surrendered, and at the same time had the ensign, which was still flying at our main-mast head, hauled down and burnt. Thereupon the Sydney ceased to fire." [41]

Von Mueller provides yet another version of events: "The commander of the *Sydney* Captain Glossop, afterwards gave me the following explanation of the firing. After the *Emden* had sent the Morse-signal "No signal-book aboard," he had twice asked us by Morse-signal "Do you surrender?" This was either not seen or not understood aboard the *Emden*. As he had no reply, and the ensign was still flying at the masthead, and no white flag was shown, he believed that the *Emden* wanted to continue the fight, and therefore gave the order to fire. This explanation cannot be considered a very sound one when one remembers that the *Emden* during the last phase of the fight had been unable to fire her guns any more, that she was lying a wreck on the reef, and that by her signal "No signal-book aboard" it was implied that she was ready to negotiate. I can I think say that in his place I should not have behaved so, but that I should have sent a boat to the *Em-*

den, probably under a flag of truce. I had also the impression that the whole transaction was later on very painful to Captain Glossop himself, and that he had let himself be persuaded into the affair mainly by his first officer." [42]

These conflicting versions of events may in part be due to the confusion and smoke of the battle, and from having been written later, when information from other sources could be included. According to Von Mueller, once the Emden was grounded, it was clear the battle was over, yet Sydney continued to bombard her. But to the British, she had not fired any torpedoes, and the crew were still armed; the ship still had not surrendered, so the battle had to continue. It should also be remembered that The Sydney still had to deal with other German vessels in the area, possible more raiders, before returning to her place with the convoy. She could not afford to either take risks or to waste time.

There was a long tradition in both navies not to surrender. "...only a few days earlier off Coronel the *Nurnberg* had fired on the defenceless *Monmouth* in exactly similar circumstances and no British officer or writer has ever complained of the act." [43] The British Official   Historian even defended the German behaviour "Had the Monmouth chosen to surrender, she could easily have done so. ... As it was, there was no choice for The Nuernberg to give her the only end she would accept. ... The Nuernberg had to make but one more run, pouring in a lacerating fire at point blank range, and then the defiant British cruiser capsized. To the end her flags were flying, and still flew as she went down. " [44]

Bunkin: *It was then approaching dusk so our Captain sent one of the German officers in one of the Buresk's boats and a German sailor with orders from our Captain if he would surrender (Captain von Mueller) then for humanity's sake he would take them all on board, if not he would leave them to their fate. We then shoved off as we did not know if there were any other cruisers in the vicinity as high power W/T activity had been heard all (the) time during the action.*

It is not clear what was causing this wireless activity, but *The Konigsberg* had not been located, and the ships may have been hunting in company, so the danger to the Sydney and to the convoy was still very real.

Von Muecke watched the battle from Direction Island and his account of the above events again causes problems: he claimed the running battle began at 8.30 am and continued for no less than 10 hours. "At sunset the Sidney ceased firing, and was seen coming back on a north-westerly course. The Emden was steering toward the east. Gradually the distance between the ships grew greater and greater, until at last they were beyond the reach of each other's guns. The fight was over.

The sun set. Darkness fell. Like a black shroud the night settled down upon both ships. "[45]

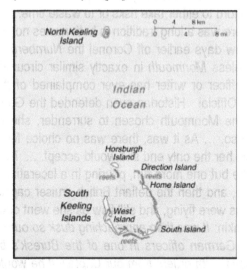

North Keeling was well out of sight of Direction Island, but he was not one to let facts ruin a good story. He claimed the Emden did "marvellously well. Unarmoured, less speedy, considerably smaller, and carrying much less heavy guns ... she maintained the battle for nearly half a day, until darkness put an end to it." [46]

After the Battle

The Times' officer reported the Sydney had suffered little damage. "The shell that exploded in the boys' mess deck, apart from ruining the poor little beggars' clothes, proved a magnificent stock of trophies. The only important damage was the after control platform, which is one mass of gaping holes and tangled iron"

One of these 'little beggars' was Henry Wilson, one of four boys from Dubbo who had joined The Sydney via The Tingira. After the war he worked as a fettler on the NSW railways, and carried mementoes of the Sydney/Emden battle with him from campsite to campsite, so they were clearly very dear to him. Unfortunately all his belongings were destroyed when his tent caught fire. [47]

Bunkin records: *We darkened the ship and started to cruise around when suddenly we heard a man's voice and as we were all eager to see where the sound came from it was not long before we saw in the distance two German sailors one supporting the other in the water, one having had his arm broken when both had been blown overboard by our gunfire. We picked them up which was not a long undertaking and placed them in the Sick Bay where they soon recovered from their Exhausted Condition 5.00 pm. We then carried on cruising and about two hours afterwards whilst cruising over the same ground we had taken during the action we heard another voice this time not so far away and we could only just discern a man on our port side. A very heavy swell was running, the lifeboat was again lowered and after struggling for about ten minutes reached the man and got him inboard and (he) immediately collapsed having been in the water for 8 hours. On the return we [were] immediately told to hoist the boat and the man was placed in the Sick Bay still unconscious but it was not long before he regained consciousness. What surprises us more than anything is the men had not been devoured by sharks as the sea is invested (sic) with them.*

We now proceed to bury our dead ... 8.00 pm the bell is told(sic) and all those not on duty is called after to the burial ser-

vice which everyone attends but with very heavy heart to think we had lost such valuable men... It is a solemn service and many a silent tear is shed as the last remains is cast into the deep. Immediately the service is over we disperse, the watch on deck to their respective duties and the watch below to turn into their hammocks for a couple of hours sleep. We then continue to cruise around during the night.

Direction Island

The Cocos islanders were alerted at 6am of the arrival of a ship at the entrance to the lagoon. They had been expecting an attack from the Emden for weeks, but the delay had given them a false sense of security. They were aware of the presence of HMAS Minotaur in the area, so when they first sighted a 4 funnelled ship approaching assumed it was her. But when they saw she flew no flags and the fourth funnel was false, so they sent off an SOS signal. At 7.30 about 50 armed Germans began approaching in boats, the station managed to send off a final signal naming the Emden and the 29 islanders became prisoners of war for the first time.

The islanders stood by whilst the raiders removed anything they could use, then destroyed equipment, even an innocuous seismograph. After several attempts, they blew up the mast, respecting locals' wishes to avoid the tennis courts but almost broke several hidden batteries instead. The water condensing plant was also spared. They intended to destroy all communications but were confused by the several dummy cables so only managed to cut the cable to Perth.

At the first explosions, and the loss of the mast, the 700 natives had 'fled incontinently to South Island in boats, bath-tubs, bailers or anything that came to hand; we understand it was a scene of indescribable panic' [48]

Questions have since been asked as to why the Emden did not bombard the island, but locals recall their unwillingness to cause harm, which fits with praise of their behaviour from the victims of their raids and the official response afterwards. Von Muller claimed "von Muecke had my orders to destroy the cable and wireless stations and if possible to cut the cables – first the Australian, next the South African, then that to the Dutch Indies. All code books and records of messages were to be brought aboard.

A recall signal was agreed on. Verbally I told ... von Mucke that, if the island was in a state of defence and garrisoned, I would give up the plan of landing and confine myself to bombarding the wireless and telegraphic stations. as a loss of personnel in this enterprise was to be avoided at all costs – this in view of the raiding campaign later on. The *Emden's* wireless had received orders to drown at once any wireless signals from the island." [49]

The two groups chatted in "pidgin English, bad German and worse Dutch". When the Germans were told that all their officers and some of the men had been awarded Iron Crosses, they replied "they'd have to be smothered in Iron Crosses to compensate them for what they'd gone through during their three months' hide and seek at sea." [50]

When the Emden raiding party saw the Sydney approaching at high speed, "...the officers whistled up their men, who straggled down to the jetty variously encumbered with bundles of old message files, a waste paper-basket of old slips, guns, books etc. We accompanied them down to the jetty, whence they embarked with no show of haste or even orderliness." [51]

Von Muecke's version is rather different and far less plausible. After 2 hours the landing party had almost completed its work when "the Emden signalled by searchlight: "Hurry your work." Almost immediately after the signal had been given, the Emden sounded her siren. This meant danger. Our men of the landing squad saw the Emden suddenly weigh anchor, turn, and run out of the harbour. The attempt made by our boats to overtake their ship by striking the shortest course toward her, although it led directly across the reef, proved of no avail." [52]

According to the islanders, the landing party got only half way back to their ship when the Emden opened fire and the battle could be followed from the roofs of their buildings. The Germans returned, planted their flag, set up guns, and the islanders were again made prisoners of war, though 4 remained at liberty to watch the sea fight. Their 'embryo press correspondent' had been asleep on the beach and joined them later, making a total of 29 prisoners.

The enemies shared sandwiches and beer and sat on the roof discussing the fight "in the most friendly manner. We watched the smoke of one of the ships on the horizon which for over an hour seemed alternately to approach and disappear, as if she were circling round but neither ship came in sight again that day." [53]

By nightfall it was clear the Emden was lost, and one of the crew asked to write a letter to his mother so the locals supplied him with writing materials "in this was felt one of those touches of Nature which make the whole world kin be he Teuton or Tasmanian, but a touch which is better understood by Exiles than by more Home staying birds"[54]

The Germans commandeered Governor Sydney Clunies-Ross's 3 masted schooner, The Ayesha. They took half the island's supplies, promising to arrange payment, and old clothes, and quite literally sailed off into the sunset "she might have formed the frontispiece to one of Robert Louis Stevenson's books," [55] They told the cable staff at Cocos they were heading towards German East Africa when they were really heading to Padang in Indonesia.

Von Muecke claimed that he commandeered The Ayesha in order to go in search of the Emden and that they looked for it all night. Of all his outlandish claims, this is perhaps the least likely - an unarmed sailing craft, already with 50 crew, setting off on a rescue mission at night with no idea where the enemy was. Locals claimed The Ayesha could not have gone far "as the breeze was very light and her best speed "before the wind" is but 8 knots.

With her launch and 2 cutters in tow it is doubtful she made more than 2." [56] It was feared that she might return or seize another ship for their escape. According to Bunkin, they were heading for the nearest neutral port, but *nothing more was heard of them until some months after and rumour reached us that they had arrived at one of the Dutch Islands in the East India Archipelago and there was interned.*

The reality was far more exciting. Von Muecke later wrote a book of their improbable journey through hostile regions in 'The Ayesha, A Great Adventure' in which they battled their way home, travelling by boats, and trains to return to Germany almost 6 months later, and were feted as war heroes.

Relieved at the German's departure, though exhausted and without lights, the islanders set to work to restore communications, and managed to speak to Singapore by 9pm. The next morning when they were communicating with Rodrigues, a cruiser was spotted and the Chinese took to the bush. Spotters on the roof soon identified the ship to be the Sydney "spick and span as if she had just returned from a naval review." [57]

As the Sydney had no idea if more raiders were in the

area, they had spent the night cruising the area. Bunkin wrote of the islanders: *Nov 10 – 30 miles away from where we left the SMS Emden found us off Direction Island at daybreak. All praise must be given to the quickness and coolness on the part of the W/T operator stationed here, for it was he who observed the Emden under disguise. While they were preparing for coaling the dummy funnel fell down by accident thus giving her away ....The operator had no sooner started to send out the message when he found he was jammed but the Emden's operator was too slow as the message had been received by the Melbourne as well as ourselves.* Here Bunkin was wrong. One record said the operator incorrectly identified the vessel as the Miinotaur. The first to sight the ship was probably the doctor with his field glasses.

Aftermath

Although Von Mueller had been told the Sydney would return the following day, he was less certain, as he expected von Muecke and his landing party to defend Direction Island, though there is no suggestion that this was ever considered by his men. He also had doubts about whether rescue boats would be able to reach his wreck through the surf and coral reefs. [58]

The Sydney sent 2 cutters and 30 men under a white flag ashore shore to find the Direction Island station free of Germans.

[we] took on board the landing party also Dr Allerhead, Dr Chadwell and Mr Ross (Photographer) as we had asked for assistance and they had volunteered their services and we must thank them for so nobly answering the appeal. We ev+entually crossed over and reached North Keeling Island where we found the Emden with a distress signal flying. Our Captain then sent a German officer with some of their men over to tell Capt von Mueller if he should give his parole he would take all the wounded on board which he agreed to. Previous to this the Officers taken of the Buresk would not give their parole but as soon as their captain gave his they also gave theirs. We immediately commenced to taken aboard the wounded, what a ghastly sight. A scene one could never forget.

The Sydney set off again at 9.30 am The Times' correspondent went to the Emden to negotiate the parole with the captain and rescue the injured. He praised the German for his fighting, was thanked but noted, "You were very lucky in shooting away all my voice-pipes at the beginning" [59] But this seems to be balanced by the loss of the Sydney's rangefinder. Strangely no author ever mentions the effect of the absent German crew, on board the 2 colliers and the many prize ships, and the 50 who were ashore, so about 1/5 of the total.

Once the first boats with the injured left, the correspondent looked round the wreck. "I have no intention of describing what I saw. With the exception of the forecastle, which is hardly touched from the forebridge to the forecastle, she is nothing but a shambles, and the whole thing most shocking."[60] This last is an interesting choice of word, also used by the Cocos Island doctor in the old English term for the butcher's area of a market. 'Dead bodies and dismembered limbs were everywhere and in corners masses of dead were immovably jammed. The ship was hard on the reef, and looked as if some gigantic hand had squeezed the life from her. ...Many were severely blistered by the fumes of the picric acid from our shells. Boat load after boat load was fetched from the stranded ship to the shore, whilst the dead floated around them." [61]

The senior medical officer's report included "All available stretchers, hammocks, and cots were sent to the Emden with a party, under Dr Ollerhead, who did not return until the last patient left the Emden some 5 hours later. Even then some Germans who had got ashore could not be brought off until the following day. The transhipping was an exceedingly difficult and painful undertaking as there was a large surf running on the beach where the Emden went ashore, and she was so much of a shambles that the shifting, collecting, and lowering of the wounded into the boats was necessarily rough.... One German surgeon, Dr Luther, was intact, but he had been unable to do much, and for a short time was a nervous wreck, having had 24 hours with so many wounded on a battered ship with none of his staff left and very few dressings, lotions and appliances. ...

Men were lying killed and mutilated in heaps, with large blackened flesh wounds. One man had a horizontal section of the head taken off, exposing mangled brain tissue. The ship was riddled with gaping holes, and it was with difficulty one could walk about the decks, and she was gutted with fire. Some of the men who were brought off to the *Sydney* presented horrible sights, and by this time the wounds were practically all foul and stinking and maggots ¼ inch long, were crawling over them, i.e. only 24 to 30 hours after injury. Practically nothing had been done to the wounded sailors, and they were roughly attended by our party and despatched to us as quickly as possible."[62] Also worthy of note is how well the exhausted surgeons operated in difficult conditions "The operations carried out under those exceptional conditions were so expertly done that in nearly all cases nothing remained for the land hospitals but to continue the regular dressings and attention." [63]   This was confirmed by Corvette Captain R Witthoeft, "The treatment which we received aboard the Australian cruiser was unquestionably good.. both the doctors and their attached personnel wore themselves almost to the bone." [64]

Both the Sydney and the Emden had two medical officers. The Emden's assistant surgeon "had been blown overboard during the action, reached North Keeling, lay exhausted all night in agonies of thirst, and in the morning drank salt water and died raving. The chief surgeon, Dr Luther, therefore found himself alone for nearly 24 hours in a battered ship with hundreds of badly wounded men, whom he had to attend without any assistance, and with a very scanty supply of dressings and appliances. It is hardly to be wondered at that, when the *Sydney* arrived, he was for a short time a nervous wreck. What is truly impressive, is that he rallied so quickly, as he was able to take over as anaesthetist when Dr Ollerhead left. [65]

The above emphasises the unusual nature of this battle – each side had traditions of refusing to surrender in defeat, so crews often went down with their ships, leaving very few injured in need of rescue and medical aid. In the aftermath of this battle, the treatment of this unusually large number of injured was often raised. "...the long but unavoidable delay in attending them - 24 hours' exposure under tropical conditions without alleviation – greatly increased both the suffering of her wounded and the difficulty of dealing with their injuries when help arrived. Both sides levelled accusations at each other in the American press – "German statements that their wounded were abandoned or maltreated, alleged British counter-charges that the German surgeons were incompetent and neglectful." [66]

As soon as all the wounded were on board we then took off the prisoners who had escaped injury. It must be said that the transporting of the wounded was the most difficult task owing to such a heavy swell and made it dangerous to them and ourselves also. The boat that brought back the news of Capt von Muller's surrender also sent a plea for water and only those who witnessed them when the water was given them can have any idea what real thirst is like. The last to leave the Emden was Capt Von Mueller and immediately he got on board and nothing more could be done to the Emden we then circled the island to find a lee shore where we could send a party to search the island should any have been washed ashore.

Before leaving his ship, the captain "with the help of a few of the officers, petty officers and crew fired the forward part of the ship in the 'tween-decks and the battery deck, after pouring over it turpentine and oil, of which, fortunately, we had a very small stock. The ship was still burning next morning but my hope that she would be quickly and completely destroyed was unfortunately not fulfilled. " [67]

Finding a favourable spot we sent in one boat one German Officer and 5 men with stretchers and water...[and several

37

others] After they had walked about 5 miles across the island they came across the bodies of some dead and some wounded. During this proceeding as it got dark we left them and cruised around all night and left them to do the best they could to bury the dead and bring the wounded to where the boats were. Of those who landed what horrible tales they told of how they found the numerous dead that was on the beach, some in praying attitude, others laid with their arms about each others neck. Others holding photos of some one dear to them, but worst of all, most of them were more or less eaten away by land crabs.

Except for cruising and keep watch now and again the night passed uneventful after we buried Reg Sharp (gunlayer) died from wounds.

Nov 11 Daybreak found us off the island and both cutters are sent in with as much assistance as possible and on arrival found the landing party of last night had returned and was waiting to bring off four seriously wounded and in decomposed state and 3 slightly wounded and immediately they were got on board and boat hoisted we then sailed for Direction Island to discharge the Drs and assistants whose services had been greatly appreciated. As soon as they got on shore and the boats back again and hoisted we then made for Colombo 11.00 am. The following day, at 1.30 pm we were making all haste to Colombo we sighted "Empress of Asia" and ordered her to close while communication was being made and ordered her to Keeling Island to carry out previous orders. (Also) to keep a sharp lookout for schooner "Ayesha" armed, also to dismantle everything of any service aboard the Emden.

On 18 November the Empress of Asia visited the Emden, to see 4 dead officers on the bridge, and elsewhere the dead piled up in great heaps. They also found men on shore, a mile or more inland, who had 'with the animal instinct, had crawled into the bush to die.' The Empress was replaced by the HMS Cadmus to make an official report, probably the first examination of the effect of modern shell fire in action, yet another first for this affair. [68]

"The wreck of the Emden was visited shortly after the departure of the Sydney by the auxiliary cruiser 'Empress of Japan' which bought away the signal log and other mementoes. At the end of November and again the following January, the wreck was inspected by H.M.S. Cadmus. In 1915 a Japanese firm offered to repair and refloat her, and the little Protector was sent off to report on her condition and salvage such guns &c as might be recoverable. The wreck, however, was already too battered by the waves to admit of refloating; and a visitor to the Cocos group in 1919 reported that almost all traces of the Emden had disappeared. [69] The wreck of the Emden is submerged on a coral reef near North Keeling Island. It was salvaged by a Japanese firm in 1960 and is now listed as a historic shipwreck. [70]

Steaming to Colombo

After the Sydney's departure, the convoy had continued on its way. By 11.15 am the convoy received the message "*Emden* beached to avoid sinking." The Minotaur then resumed her course away from the convoy. The *Konigsberg* threat continued for another night and day until news was received that it had been sighted on the African coast, so the region was free of enemy ships. [71]

On board the Sydney, the Doctors and their assistants worked endlessly as they rushed towards Colombo for proper medical facilities. Early in the morning of November 13 they sighted the cruiser Empress of Russia, who gave the Sydney some medical supplies and took all the prisoners who could be moved, so improving conditions on board. On November 15 the Sydney passed through the ANZAC convoy to anchor at Colombo, where all the wounded were transferred to hospital. Uninjured survivors of the Emden were distributed among the convoy, to be taken to Malta as prisoners of war. [72]

Nov 15 5.00 pm Passed through the convoy who by orders of signal were told not to cheer and who adhered to the signal until the last ship was reached. It just seemed the men could not retain their enthusiasm any longer and with one huge cheer they greeted us again and again until we were out of hearing. We proceeded into harbour and immediately we had secured to the buoy transport lighters came alongside for the wounded and we discharge them ashore. What a sight, our own lads are as cheerful as can be (although some are seriously wounded) and set an example of how a true Britisher can fight and suffer for his country's sake without murmuring.

The gratitude of the troops was a taste of what was to follow. The Sydney was soon passing 40 to 50 ships per day, showing how much shipping had been held up.

The Sydney then passed through the Suez Canal, with Bunkin full of wonder at the hundreds of camels in pens, sandbag fortifications and *'the famous regiments of Sikhs who have always carried a high standard of efficiency with them and it is indeed a pleasure to gaze upon such a smart lot of men who carry discipline out to the letter. .... A picture surely no artist could paint'.* After passing an expanse of desert, they see rows of tents and sentries of the Yorkshire & Lancashire Regiment.

'We had almost let this scene slip from us when we saw two or three making down towards the edge of the canal and as we draw up to them one called out

"Is that the Sydney?"

A silence for two or three seconds that could almost be felt, then in a voice only just heard one of our boys said "Yes" and immediately a rousing cheer went up and it just seemed as if the tents became alive. Before one could collect his thoughts and views of the scenery that presented itself hundreds of soldiers mustered on the bank of the canal and we heard a distant order given

"Three cheers for HMAS Sydney Officers and Men"

This the lads did in true style. Our Commander who was on the bridge called out

"Three cheers for the York and Lancashire"

and this we did to a man.

We had no sooner passed these men than we came in line with their horses, hundreds of them feeding, some laying down but all ready to move at a moments notice should the enemy attempt on any part to block the canal by filling it in. As we pass another space of desert confronts us and then again we come in view of more tents and still more tents belonging to the Y & L. We gradually let this view pass from us and now we see nothing again but desert on both sides of us. It is now about midnight and we expect to arrive at Port Said very early hours of the morning so it is scarce the trouble to catch a few hours sleep.'

Arriving at the war zone, they look down on rows of trenches with machine guns and heavy artillery....This is surely war to its utmost!

We are now gradually passing this scene but we are not going to get past without a cheer. The commanding officer is seen to run along the parapet of the trenches and the order is given

"3 cheers for HMAS Sydney Captain Glossop officers and men"

With a feel almost like thunder, 3 cheers come from the Y & L in trenches and we again acknowledge them as we gradually glide away from this scene. We, one and all, are a little more contented at having seen what trench life is like.

News Spreads

There is much of this story which clearly belongs to another, more civilised age, none more so than the attitude of the victors towards their victims. It is refreshing to read war reports that are free of the malice of the modern media. The press and public piled praise on both the Sydney and the Emden crews.

Stevenson recorded :"Captain von Mueller dispatched his command during this difficult time with honour. His crew suffered horrendous casualties and instead of sinking his ship he deliberately drove her aground on a reef in order to save the wounded from drowning. The Emden was posthumously awarded the Iron

Cross for valour.. and all subsequent ships of the name show the Iron Cross on their bow." [73]

The London Telegraph response is unimaginable today: "It is almost in our hearts to regret that the Emden has been captured and destroyed. There is not a survivor who does not speak well of this young German, the officers under him and the crew obedient to his orders. The war on the sea will lose some of its piquancy, its humour and its interest now that the Emden has gone."

The Emden's demise was reported on page 8 of the London Times on November 11, followed by the detailed report by the Sydney's officer on December 15, including a map of the running battle. In Bombay the announcement was made at a dinner party for leading citizens "The commercial destruction of the Emden has been so troublesome to Indian trade and her exploits so disturbed timid Indian capitalists that the news that her career had ended caused great satisfaction." Whilst it is easy to mock the cowardice of the colonial merchants, ships carried men and essential supplies. Bunkin's diary repeatedly mentions the hundreds of tons of coal which took hours to load, often injuring the crew, and then the ship needed to be cleaned, a reminder of how fragile were the lines of communication and trade which held the empire together.

World leaders were fulsome in their praise of the bravery of the crew of the Sydney.

"Warmest congratulations on brilliant entry of Royal Australian Navy to the war." First Lord of the Admiralty

"While not only appreciating to the full protection afforded to British communities in the Pacific by Australian section of Imperial Navy, we are all proud of splendid services rendered to Empire by your fine ships and their gallant seamen." – Prime Minister of New Zealand

The Times correspondent agreed with Prince Hohenzolern 'it was our job to knock one another out, but there was no malice in it.'

Officially 115 died and 80 were injured on the Emden, 4 died and 8 injured on the Sydney.

Epilogue

Edward Bunkin's journal continued its daily log of infuriatingly brief snippets for the remainder of his tour. They spent much time cruising the Caribbean, occasionally escorting ships, but mostly investigating maritime traffic. As a lay preacher he made a lot of friends in the Salvation Army and the Wesleyans during many trips ashore, especially in Jamaica. He preached a few times and once gave a talk for an hour forty minutes on "Sydney's part from the outbreak of war". What a pity no copy of this survives.

By midnight 3 August 1916 he noted the Sydney had covered 101,117 miles. After some bad weather, he noted *'The sea is still very heavy and the man who wrote that "Long Rolling Home to Merry England" must have had an idea what bad weather is like. Different to the man who penned those words "A Life on the Ocean Wave".*

The journal ended on 16 September 1916 with 'enter Plymouth 11.45 pm ties to no. 6 buoy."

Edward Bunkin (1881-1961)

Edward was born in Dublin where he married Ada St Clair Quick. He trained as a carpenter and signed on with the Royal Navy in 1901 for 12 years. In 1907 he was promoted to shipwright and soon after signed up for a further 10 years when this journal began. He was discharged with a pension in June 1922. He spent his retirement in Plymouth where he kept an allotment. He named his son Sydney.

He had a deeply evangelical but not intrusive Christian faith, was a good singer and a lay preacher. When his messmates went carousing ashore at various ports he was more likely to be drinking tea at the local mission. Edward was very fond of children and his youngest grandson Derek who transcribed his journal has fond memories of him in old age.

HMAS Sydney I

In May 1917 the Sydney was involved in possibly the most futile battle ever—with several other ships in the Firth of Forth, trying to bring down a Zeppelin which was well above the range of her guns, whilst the ships were too fast for the airship to hit. Later that year she gained a Sopwith Ships Pup fighter with launching platform. She was present when the German High Seas' Fleet surrendered on 19 July 1919 and remained in service till 1928. Parts of her are distributed in various memorials around Sydney including the mast at Bradley's Head and the bow blended into the base of the Harbour Bridge.

Captain J T G Glossop (1871-1934)

He served in Australian waters from his late teens, and had a long and distinguished association with the Royal Australian Navy. He became an international celebrity as a result of this battle, a town in South Australia is named after him and he became a Companion of the Bath, the Japanese Order of the Rising Sun and the French Legion d'Honneur.

Captain K F M von Mueller (1873-1923)

He was awarded the Iron Cross First Class after the battle, and was separated from his crew and imprisoned in the midlands where he led a failed escape. Weakened by malaria, he was sent to the Netherlands for treatment then repatriated home.

Lieut. Helmuth Von Muecke (1881-1957)

He was the most famous and controversial of the survivors. He wrote best selling accounts of the battle and their return. He was an active journalist until banned and twice imprisoned by the Nazis. His son died in World War II and he later opposed his country's rearmament and campaigned for peace.

References

[1] p.1 'Before Gallipoli – Australian Operations in 1914' in Semaphore, Newsletter of the Sea Power Centre Australia Issue 7, August 2003

[2] p.3-4 Cocos (Keeling) Islands Historical Society Journal Newsletter, Vol 1 Issue 4]

[3] p.1 www.gunplot.net/ww1/ww1.html

[4] p.186 Arthur W Jose, 'Official Histories – first World War Volume IX – the Royal Australian Navy, 1914-1918' (9th edition, 1941) from ww.awm.gov.au/histories/chapter.asp – hereafter Official Histories

[5] p.150 Official Histories

[6] p.153 Official Histories

[7] p.154 Official Histories

[8] footnote p.179 Official Histories

[9] 'Alfred Shout- Australia's Most Decorated Hero at Gallipoli' updated 2 march 2003 www.firstworldwar.com/features/shutvc.htm

[10] p.164 Official Histories

[11] p.180/1 Official Histories

[12] p.203/3 Official Histories

[13] p.3 'Australia's First Naval Fight November 1914' the Military Historical Society of Australia 1978 (first published 1915)

[14] p.179 Official Histories

[15] p.155 Official Histories

[16] HH Harmes-Emden Tribute to Emden Commander]

[17] p.93-4 Kapitaenleutnant von Muecke, 'The Emden' trans Helene S. White, Ritter & Co. Boston Mass 1917

[18] p.167 Official Histories

[19] www.worldwar1.co.uk/emden.html

[20] p.168 Official Histories

[21] p.219, Maria Weinand, translated Margarete Muensterberg in 'The Emden'

[22] footnote p 168 Official Histories

[23] p.95 'The Emden'
[24] p.124-7 'The Emden'
[25] p.122/3 'The Emden'
[26] p.42 'The Emden'
[27] p.182/3 'The Emden'
[28] p.193 Official Histories
[29] p.179 Official Histories
[30] p.193 Official Histories
[31] p.194 Official Histories
[32] p.182 Official Histories
[33] p.2 Captain von Mueller's Report to the German Admiralty, translated from Krieg zur See 1914-18 "Der Kreuzer Krieg" www.gwpda.org/naval/emden.htm hereafter von Mueller's Report
[34] p.181 Official Histories
[35] p.182 Official Histories
[36] p.185 Official Histories
[37] 'The Last fight of the Emden. Vivid Account by an Officer of the Sydney' in p8 London Times, Tuesday December 15 1914
[38] p.5 von Mueller's Report to the Admiralty
[39] p.130 Phil Andere, 'The Cocos Coup. The Real History of the "Emden's" Raid & Capture' in The Zodiac – The Magazine of the Cable & Wireless Company Vol 8 June 1914-16
[40] Report of Captain John C.T. Glossop, of the Sydney www.blakearchive.org.uk/mirrors/www.lib.byu.edu:80/~rdh/wwi/1914/emden.html
[41] p.6 Von Mueller's report
[42] ditto
[43] p.189 Official Histories
[44] footnote p.189 Official Histories
[45] p.215 'The Emden'
[46] p.217 'The Emden'

[47] Information from Kevin Wilson, grandson of Henry Wilson who was a 16 year old on board the Sydney
[48] p.131 'The Zodiac '
[49] Von Mueller's report
[50] p.128 'The Zodiac'
[51] p.129 'the Zodiac'
[52] p.208 'The Emden'
[53] p.132 The Zodiac'
[54] do
[55] p.133 'The Zodiac'
[56] do
[57] do
[58] p.201 Official Histories
[59] London 'Times' as above
[60] ditto
[61] p.134 'The Zodiac'
[62] Dr Leonard Darby 'The Post-Action Report of the Senior Medical Officer of HMAS Sydney after the Engagement with SMS Emden' www.vlib.us/medical/darby/darby.htm
[63] p.193 Official Histories
[64] 'Unsere Emden' p.273 quoted in p 202 footnote Official Histories
[65] p.190/1 Official Histories
[66] p.192 Official Histories
[67] p.201 Official Histories
[68] p.135 'The Zodiac'
[69] p.207 Official Histories
[70] www.geocities.com/pumbo99/battle_1.html?200822
[71] p.203 Official Histories
[72] p.202 Official Histories
[73] p.4 Cocos (Keeling) Islands Historical Society Journal Vol 1 issue 4 p.4